To Bev ...
SO-DTA-425

A Time Of Trial

Beyond the Terror of 9/11

Editor
Katherine L. Gordon

Copyright © 2001 Book – Hidden Brook Press

Copyright © 2001 Poetry – Authors

All rights for poems revert to the authors. All rights for book and layout remain with Hidden Brook Press. No part of this book may be reproduced except by a reviewer who may quote brief passages in a review. The use of any part of this publication reproduced, transmitted in any form or by any means, electronic, mechanical, photocopied, recorded or otherwise stored in a retrieval system without prior written consent of the publisher is an infringement of the copyright law.

Editor – Katherine L. Gordon
Copy Editor – Kim Grove
Layout and Design – Richard M. Grove
Cover Design – Christopher R. Grove
Cover Art – Richard M. Grove

Printed and bound in Canada 2000

National Library of Canada Cataloguing in Publication Data

Main entry under title:
        A time of trial : beyond the terror of 9/11

Includes CD-ROM.
Includes bibliographical references.
ISBN 1-894553-30-6

   1. September 11 Terrorist Attacks, 2002--Poetry. 2. Canadian poetry (English)—21st century. 3. American poetry—21st century.
I. Gordon, Katherine L.

PS8287.S46T55 2001   C811'.6080358   C2001-904308-2
PR9195.85.S46T55 2001

**Published by
Hidden Brook Press
412 - 701 King Street West
Toronto, Ontario, Canada M5V 2W7
(416) 504-3966
writers@hiddenbrookpress.com
http://www.hiddenbrookpress.com**

Forward From The Red Cross

The Canadian Red Cross Society extends its congratulations and thanks to Richard Grove of Hidden Brook Press and the many talented authors who so generously donated their work for inclusion in Time of Trial. We also extend our thanks to the generous corporate sponsors whose financial support made the publication of this book possible as a fundraiser for the Red Cross USA Appeal.

During times of crisis, people turn to each other in a common humanity. September 11, 2001 will be etched in our minds forever. These poems echo the breadth of human emotion - heart break, despair, anger and more importantly love, tolerance and hope for a future free of hatred and war. It is this call for tolerance, understanding and respect among all people that truly reflects the basic principles of the Red Cross.

For over 140 years, a red cross on a white background, the reverse of the Swiss flag in honor of our founder, Henri Dunant, has been a symbol of help and hope during people's darkest hour. In response to the tragedy of September 11th, over 46,000 American Red Cross disaster services personnel - 43,000 of them volunteers, provided victims and rescue workers with shelter, meals, tracing and reunion services as well as counseling and psychological support. Funds were provided to families of the victims to cover travel and funeral expenses. Canadian Red Cross volunteers helped 33,000 airplane passengers diverted to Canadian airports, where they were stranded for days, while others assisted highway travelers caught for days by tightened security at border crossings.

Proceeds from the sale of this book will be used to provide direct assistance to the victims of the September 11th tragedy. The American Red Cross has extended its Family Gift Program which provides financial assistance to families of the victims to cover expenses such as rent or mortgage payments, healthcare, utility bills and counseling. Red Cross was there to assist immediately after the tragedy and will continue to be there to support families of the victims into the future, thanks to the overwhelming support of generous donors from around the world.

Lois Flemming
Director Fund Development
The Canadian Red Cross Society

Editor's Note

It has been both an honour and a challenge to receive words from around the world and unite them meaningfully in this impactful volume. The poems collected here express a range of emotion and perception as only poetry can do.

We offer them as part of the quest for an insightful global healing.

Katherine L. Gordon,
Editor

Thank You

I would like to thank Katherine Gordon, a dear friend and fellow member of the Canadian Poetry Association executive, for her instant willingness to take on the daunting task of being editor for this book.

Thank you, Gloria MacDonald, from PostLinx for helping me to coordinate some of the corporate partners. Your help filled in the gaps that I did not have time to take care of.

I would like to thank Peter Dalglish of Ridpath's Fine Furniture for being the first person to believe in the project with financial support. Thank you for your on-going support of Hidden Brook Press and Canadian poetry in general. You have helped to bring poetry to the world.

I would like to thank all of the corporate partners that helped to make this project possible: The Globe and Mail for their support as media sponsor, PostLinx for taking care of the mailing of the many thousands of books, Indas for taking care of the credit card ordering on line, Allard Creative Communications for webdesign, EarthFish Productions for the CD ROM design and for filming the documentary, Grove Graphic Design for the fine book cover, thanks Chris. I would also like to thank Transcontinental for the fine job they did on printing the book.

Thank you Oasis at 294 College Street, Toronto for providing the space free for us to have our prelaunch reading and shoot the documentary that is on the CD ROM. Also thank you Michael Connolly for doing the interviews for the documentary.

Everyone has worked without pay on this project from Hidden Brook Press on down the line. Thank you all.

Richard M. Grove,
Project Director

Forward From The Publisher

It was amazing how many submissions flooded in from around the world on the topic of the September 11, 2001 bombing tragedy in the United States. It should hardly be a surprise that poetry is a significant creative release for the accomplished, as well as for the previously published poet. Many turned to pen as the events actually unfolded, triggered into action with numb disbelief. Others wrote days and weeks later with a more gentle reflective retrospect; what an incredible selection arrived at our email address.

When we first put out a call for submissions to the general public I expected some seventy-five to one hundred poems to be submitted and that wc would publish a small anthology. This was not to be the case; with the instantaneous power of the internet we were flooded with submissions within hours. Within two days we had surpassed our expectations of one hundred submissions and within a week had exceeded five hundred. The tidal wave seemed to wain just a bit over the following days as we topped over seven hundred submissions from around the world but by the end of the allocated two week submission period we received well over one thousand submissions from Australia, Canada, Denmark, France, Hawaii, Hungary, India, Malaysia, Nigeria, Portugal, South Africa, United Arab Emirates, United Kingdom, USA and Zimbabwe. What an amazing creative surge. I can only wonder how many poems might have poured in if we had left the submission deadline open for longer.

This anthology is a tremendous example of what People's Poetry is all about, the personal heart-felt expression of what is turning in the minds of the masses. In this light I truly hope that you enjoy the reflections of inspired brothers and sisters from around the world.

Richard M. Grove,
Project Director

Dedication

THE AFTERMATH

Dear Readers:

With the tragic events,
that have occurred,
over the past few days,
with the dust that will not settle,
it is vital to us all,
that we express in a poetic collective voice,
of love, and compassion
our deep sadness and sympathies,
to all of those affected.

While it seems so little,
to offer,
in the front of such,
incomprehensible loss,
please know that our thoughts,
and our prayers,
are with you all,
all in this global city,
during this painful time.

With respect and sadness
Sincerely,
Your brother
Richard M. Grove

Table of Contents

Chapter One – Architecture Of The Heart

Chapter Two – An Ascension Of Ashes

Chapter Three – Of Elegies And Aftermath

Chapter Four — Weeds Of War Blossoms Of Brotherhood

Chapter One
Architecture Of The Heart

John B. Lee – Brantford, Ontario, Canada
UNTIL THE STARS THAT ARE NOT THERE HAVE DISAPPEARED

I am in a line up
on the stairs
descending
from the stars that are not there.

My face has burned a window passing
as does the frost
as does the ghost of dust
that's left from the millenary faith of moths in light.
Mine are the shadows
that haunt the lazy glass beneath the glare.
Mine are the gauzy webs
of a wedding
when the bride has married sorrow
to a spider skein
and kept unending vigil
with an attic veil.
My visage swims the sticky spinnerets
drowned sailors find
in deep repose
as fishermen haul forth from fathoms
their weighty death
where mermaids flag their fins
and slip away from grief.
I am in a line
upon the stairs
descending
from the stars that are not there.

I shall not step
lest I should fly.
I shall not step
lest I should fall.
I shall not step
until the stars that are not there
have disappeared.

J. Graham Ducker — Oshawa, Ontario, Canada
SEPTEMBER 11

Silver slashes carve
Concrete symbolic towers.
We change forever.

J. Graham Ducker — Oshawa, Ontario, Canada
ANGUISH

Iron and rock pyres
Still billow incessantly,
While hope drifts away

Leda Lubynskyj — Toronto, Ontario, Canada
UNTITLED

I, who almost never cry,
Cry now for strangers
And a mile of fractured rock.

I, who almost never pray,
Pray now with heated indignation
Demanding miracles
Of God:

Find this man's son,
This woman's daughter,
This husband, this uncle, this friend;
Find this man who was admired,
This woman who was loved,
This timid youth whom
Almost no one knew
(Last seen diminishing
In waves of oily smoke).

Find...find...
Find more than limbs,
Than shattered fragments of mortality,
Find faith, find hope,
Find love and charity
This Tuesday, September 11, 2001.

Linda Rogers — Victoria, British Columbia, Canada

911

The old wives told us to catch a bird
you had to pour salt on its tail.
While swallows tumble and free fall,
laughing at their tender view of a world
in nuclear winter, snow falling everywhere,
some feathered pilots land on the plump
bodies of earthworms coming up for air
on sunny mornings like this, when all
should be right with a world washed clean
by sudden lightning and rain. Morning Has Broken,
is that the song for a day like this,
when you wake up from a dream and tell me
you heard temple bells, and saw Valkyries
carrying soldiers away from the fields of war?

In your sleep, you met a veiled woman
who told you to put salt on it to prevent
something terrible from happening.
"Salt on what?" you wondered before
we heard the thump on the window and saw
the lifeless creature lying upside down
beside the newspaper on the porch.
"Why do they do it?" you asked, your dream
coming clear in the first wave of grief
that woke us up, before the telephone rang.
Is it because the room he was trying
to enter is the colour of Paradise,
where swallows hunt insects and animals
further down the food chain, and a Promised
Land where everyone is welcome?

What was he thinking when he saw
the moment between the air and one
room where a family gazes at the sky
and everything in it, angels and airplanes,
was made of glass? Did he think he would
change the world by smashing one window?
Was he trying to break the sound barrier,
make himself understood on the ground?
Did he consider turning away when he saw
his own reflection, or did he believe
it was still the face of God, in the
language of birds, calling him home?

Karin de Weille — Yonkers, NY, USA
IF ONLY

If only I had driven the kids and she–
If only he had taken his vacation and I–
If only our shifts–

If only the towers were empty.

If only we had seen them empty their hearts.

Oh, we emptied the buildings but not fast enough, not
fast enough

Barbara Gray — Ottawa, Ontario, Canada
TWINS

The deepest chills of winter
came in four gusts
from the east
one late summer

Four loaded darts
filled with fuel
and human cargo
their destinations planned
by two opposing forces

only one would win

Those looking skyward
watched events of un virtual reality
The planes
had been knocked off their courses
after falling
into the hands of darkness

Two were guided into
sister buildings
wherein worked a city of professionals

The first target hit its chosen
and the second followed in kind
Flames of destruction raged
and melted down
the two unprotected soldiers

Their heads toppled
they fell to their knees
then totally disintegrated
into a pile
of twisted steel and dust
Their own terrible weight

grinding out their very existence
they haunt the whole world
with ghostly memories
shifting the human perception
of security

Another hit its target
but slightly off
The fourth
found the truest form of heroism
Its path disrupted by bravery
the going down in flames kind
Smashing it into an empty field
instead of a deadly unknown

We will remember
Darkness flees from light

Bess Kemp —
NYC

the blackened skyline
is weeping ash and rain
for sorrows too numerous
to count
it all begins and ends
in the clouds
too high to see to ground
close enough to the sun
to melt like
candy

but the taste
will never be
sweet

Ryn Gargulinski — Brooklyn, NY, USA
PELIGRO MEANS DANGER

A reflection from the Coney Island Boardwalk
one whole week after the WTC disaster

Today
even the
waves are mad they
rollick against
the shore to match
my thoughts up here

on the boardwalk
people parched
with memories they either
cannot let go or will not
dare to remember

the surf churns debris

a chunk of
pier, of driftwood

could it be from
that far north
from that
jade hole in the
sky where the
sun once
was?

David Cale — Brampton, Ontario, Canada
THE BLINDING

New York
seat of wealth and power
Washington
seat of might and rule

Like Lear you sat not knowing
that the blasted heath
and the vicious blinding
would fly unbidden

Twin towers of the west
illusions of a kingdom now fallen
leaving as the new centre of our lives
an empty wilderness of the soul

And from under the desolation
we can just hear the king's wail
a millennium old
yet still echoing in storms such as these

    "Let the great gods... Find their enemies now. Tremble, wretch,
That has within thee undivulged crimes, Unwhipped of justice.
    I am more sinned against than sinning."
Here the kings and servants of commerce were slain
Those who worshipped and trusted in
the gods of wealth and power
and felt invulnerable in their fortress
The other gods look down
some cry - some laugh

The CNN anchor intones

    "Poor naked wretches, where ever you are,
    in this pitiless storm,
    How shall our houseless heads..., defend you
    From seasons such as these?

    O, we have taken too little care of this!"

Behind him
faces of those who 'spent' their lives
delivering their hate spawned by fanatic belief
brief meaning found in the free trading of
eyes for eyes
blind faith for blind faith

And so we sit in our walled up countries
the barbarian at the gate
fear in our gut feeding the hate in our hearts
transfixed by the image
of our armies attempts at retribution
flailing in the dark even with night vision
terrified that our world we thought we knew
has collapsed in ruin
leaving only rubble beneath our feet

We wonder if the poison pen
has touched our unopened mail

And we howl as Lear over his daughter's body
dead from his blind folly

> "Why should a dog, a horse, a rat, have life....
> And these no breath at all?
> They will come no more,
> Never, never, never, never, never!"

Quotes are from William Shakespeare's play "King Lear"

12

Roger Bell — Port McNicoll, Ontario, Canada
OUTSIDE KITCHENER/INSIDE NEW YORK

Outside Kitchener
north of the major highway
in a spot where brown cattle
once stood and gazed placidly
ruminated upon bovine things
the tenderness of individual blades of grass
the easy autumn sky
the swish of tails in unison

now sits a mountain of green glass
countless
windshields, back and side windows
spidered and cracked
a troll's hoard of diamonds
winking in the mid-day sun
imagine
each one containing
a thousand broken times each
the final look of doomed passengers
their longing to reverse time
before the car left the safety of its wheels
and screamed metal
 magine those on the top floors
of the World Trade Center
their princely view of the city
gone ragged
rippled with flame and smoke
their envy of the gleaming river
the far New Jersey shore
and then the groan as the towers gave themselves
up to physics and slid down
faster now, faster
the last descending looks through green glass
rushing to return itself
to the earth whence it came.

Richard M. Grove — Toronto, Ontario, Canada

The Voice of Terror: September 11, 2001

Fictional eye witness accounts

A prayer for world peace today
as the voice of terror reigns over Manhattan.
Somehow we have to be strong
as twin towers plummet to dust.
How horrific, how sad.

"It's down
it's all down
it's like an hallucination
one minute we are trying to evacuate the victims
and the next minute there is no building
it's down and rubble
it's smoke and dust
it's death."

Get ready for the numbers,
to be in the tens of thousands.
10,000 dead?
50,000 dead?
More?
Futile speculation shivers

"I came down 80 floors
thank God I'm alive
I came down the stairs
rubble
dust
debris everywhere.
I ran for my life.
I ran with the cloud of death
hissing at my heels"

The terror is being compared
to Pearl Harbour.
The movie was almost real
but the smell of popcorn
covered the stench of death.

"Everything just fell in
we clawed our way out from the rubble
over dead bodies
you needed a shovel just to breathe
I thought I was going to die
I thought I was dead."

Our freedom was under attack today,
"It was a despicable attack of cowardice",
rang from the media
hour upon hour in slow motion
til we had the lines memorized
the pain internalized.

"Let me out"
shrieks from under rubble
"Let me out
Dear God I can't breath
I'm hurt.
Please, I'm under here."

Is there any way
to make sense of destruction?
Is there any way to understand
the voice of terror?

Caroline H. Davidson — Pickering, Ontario Canada
SEPTEMBER DAY

Above the goldenrod
above white and purple asters
clear blue September sky
gulls crying over our heads

I pan the camera across the river
smoke from one of the twin towers
sound of distant plane
coming closer low overhead

my camera picks it up
follows it to the other tower

Oh, My God!!

white and purple asters
wave in the breeze

goldenrod in sunlight

gulls crying overhead

Chris Bluemer — Atlantis, Florida, USA
NO TOWERS

Like a hot bath drawn,
your being surrounded me.
Now my heart shivers.

Gene Doty — Rolla, MO, USA
GONE: A GHAZAL

After the fire and the explosions, the towers are gone,
the towers, the people, and one fifth of the Pentagon.

On the Web, the airliner moves slowly, in dream-like video,
behind the towers, where bright red blossoms, then is gone.

At home, the answering machine blinks and beeps,
a new message in my mailbox, telling me peace has gone.

Lower Manhattan wears a hijab of dust and smoke,
a veil concealing the eyes whose ease has gone.

Numerically the date is 9-1-1, an emergency call
for each of us to act before the world is gone.

A news-weekly filled with photos of rubble and death;
suddenly my appetite for news at dinner is gone.

Nearly seven thousand dead as I write:
strangers, friends, fellow-workers, family–gone.

Such a terror demands a Guernica, a death-metal raga,
not, Gino, a poet whose sense of balance has gone.

Michael Mirolla — Toronto, Ontario, Canada
STAYING AFLOAT: 11/09/2001

The sigh of a long flutter towards unyielding ground:
words shaped into paper wings
riding the bittersweet currents between canyon walls.

There are messages in mid-draft, the laundry lists
of an ancient serendipity,
bills and invoices enough for any reckoning,
deadly formulas amid the dawdles of the pure of heart.

There are temper tantrums waiting
to explode, memoranda CCed for urgent delivery,
a brace of lottery tickets in search
of new winners, lap-top love letters trapped
within viral e-mails, the tale of Narcissus
in replication's twisted mirror.

There are, in the midst of artificial intelligences,
the lost ingredients of a true understanding,
bits of code in fractal flowering,
listless pixels tap tapping their ghostly salutation
to friend and foe alike.

Commingled now, they glide on puffs
of red-hot air, oblivious to the dense gravity below,
the angry yawn of inertia.
Yet knowing all the while that sooner or later
Earth's siren call will hug them to itself,
will re-unite them with those who long before stopped
dreaming.

Elana Wolff — Thornhill, Ontario, Canada
ANGLES OF MYSTERY September 11th

"Surely all art is the result of one's having been in danger."
Carolyn Forche, The Angel of History

The apertures are open, cameras
rolling for the hit.
After attack
the playback from a dozen different views.
No
one
angle can grasp it.

Two towers.
the twin
ones of 11 implode
        Sep
        tem
        ber
        in the morning.

Away from Ground Zero, out of New York, in another country,
in a yellow kitchen,
the two l's in yellow
look a lot like the ones in 11   El even.
El   read God   is even /
fair, itself another puzzle.

Krisha Wignarajah — Ottawa, Ontario, Canada
TWIN TOWERS

Unfurl fire
somber retreat down the stairwell;
ascent on stairwell to final resurrection
Faces everywhere, then nowhere
and those fingers that try to seep through
cell phone signals into safe arms
are pulled back - no more minutes left.

Chapter Two
An Ascension Of Ashes

Katherine L. Gordon — Rockwood, Ontario, Canada

THE HARVEST OF BLACK SEPTEMBER

In the bright autumn of our year
      they fell.
Young leaves of life
who bannered our hearts
with love and joy,
their farewell a flame
that burned the innocence from our world.

Now, in their names,
from soot and ashes of mean death
we rescue their light,
unite with their astonished spirits
as they fade unwilling
from this plane.

Brothers and sisters
across the lands of earth
will transform cruelty to kindness,
will build a monument,
not of stone or steel,
but of the human spirit.

Donna Allard — Moncton, New Brunswick, Canada
THE DUST WILL NEVER SETTLE

Little Satan is Canada
Big Satan is the USA according to Bin Laden followers.
America At War September 11, 2001

~~~~~~~~~~

Little Satan watching
Paranoid and cautious
As morning flowers over NY City
Puppet planes whose strings were pulled and cut
Tore into NY's Twin Towers erupting into back draft flames
Horrors REPLAY on news casts
Cell phone silence
Workers leap in fear from buildings clouded in dust
The earth rumbles
To the rhythm of the dead
As people stand for anthems
Haunting tapping on steel defy the three minutes of silence
Memorials that are world wide
Garland this planet to wear
After this moment of nakedness
The statue of Liberty?
Standing for Freedom
As rain tears upon the handheld poem
Remembrance
Let not blood color our earth
Pope John Paul kneeling in white,
Hands upon his face in anguish,
The world is under siege
All are on alert
A silence even the dead can hear
I am calm
But scared for I know
The dust will never settle
The dust will never settle
The dust will never settle

John H. Baillie — Winnipeg, Manitoba, Canada
SEARCHING

I search for the mercy
in the eyes
closest to mine.
Turned aside.
Fearing to show
the need, the loss
of what was fragile,
unappreciated,
yearning to carry on
business as usual,
your eyes
will not meet mine.
We pass,
hearts smothered
in ugly grey ash,
your cheek turned away
hiding tears
flowing into
the unforgiving silence
of so many voices
now without words,
identity itself
overwhelmed.
So necessary now
that tender recognition
mingles our tears
to yet wash clear
the ash; face to face
to start a world
anew.
In a time
when men take action
turning planes
into living agents
of burning conflagration,
the least
that can happen here
is for my hand
to reach out
and touch yours.

Avril J. Winchester — Rockwood, Ontario, Canada
SEPTEMBER

an old man shuffles by on a warm September day
tattered coat dragging along the sidewalk
stirring the litter and dust,
eyes scanning the gutters and bins,
he watches the people hurrying by:
>tycoons, cell phones glued to their ears,
>smart women, conquerors of commerce,
>all eager to enter the twin towers
>soaring to heaven, hiding the Manhattan sky.
>The people bring gifts of skill to lay
>before the gods of trade,
>making the world a better place.
>Of every faith or non-belief
>they share a common goal,
>following a thousand years of
>trading, from all around the globe.

The old man ponders what might have been,
voices echo from memories-
"Some are born great, some achieve greatness"
He sighs, but not with bitterness;
each day he watches thousands of
shiny shoes pass by as he wiggles his
dirty toe-nail, pointing to the sky.
But to-day he wishes for a cell phone,
someone he could call,
to cry a last "I LOVE YOU"
as death explodes his sky.

Paul Carr — Toronto, Ontario, Canada
AND THE END

And the dust
it settled
on the faces
of the children
who played
in sand-boxes.

And the concrete
it settled
into the pores
and veins
of underground
filtration systems
contaminating
our blood.

And the stench
of the lies
that bellowed
from t.v. sets
spewing venom
pierced
the silence
of last rights.

And the smoke
smoldered ashes
of sacred ritual
in the name of
the almighty
sailing through
snake-infested
streams.

And the end
the end of the end
endless beginning
of the end
ending forever
another day
another way
far away
the end
never ends.

Jean M. Chard — Dartmouth, NS, Canada
THREE DAYS AFTER

The dust of the dead
has coloured this golden sunset.
I breathe their atoms
into my lungs.

Pushed into our past
before their time
by that unspeakable pyre,
did their spirits rush
up from the smoke,
a single exhalation of souls
escaping into a different life?

Richard M. Grove – Toronto, Ontario, Canada
The New Landscape

September 11th, 2001
finds two American icons crushed.
The smoke has not yet cleared
to reveal the new landscape of
"brotherhood" – all mankind reaching,
knowing that good will prevail.

There is still much rubble
to be cleared and tears to dry but
under the fallen concrete
there will be found a new landscape of
"solidarity" – all working for the ideal
of democracy rather than difference.

We all shall learn and grow spiritually
as we discover more about God
through oneness
which will inevitably reveal the new landscape of
"unity" – not distinction of race and religion
but harmony in the new tomorrow.

C.E. Chaffin —
ROUGH DRAFT
OF WORLD TRADE CENTER KADDISH
SOME EXCERPTS:

Black woman in white face.
Is this Pompeii?
No, nothing to preserve.
What happened to the skyline?
The lions still flank the library
but the pillars of Manhattan imploded,
collapsed like paper pagodas.
And the ash survivors wear
contains the victims.
Fire makes us one.
Have mercy, God.

****

Back in D.C. the impenetrable fortress
looks like someone cut a slice of pizza from it.
Yet it stands. Worse is the memory
of that space no longer occupied,
where all the sudden ghosts
have nothing to haunt save a pit of debris--
no fax machines, no wheeled chairs,
no filing cabinets, no lights,
no basement and no roof.

How many ways of not approaching
this atrocity, this public violation?
America, you have been put in stocks
for all the world to see..
Oceans and friends no longer protect you.

Jackie Cleveland — Harpersville, AL, USA
FOR JUST A MOMENT

dust of the ages
blew a different way
far from the routine
endless telemarketers,
card-chewing ATMs,

frenzied shopping,
and fast foods
when fanatical fliers
shattering
skyscrapers
put all senses on hold.

I finally wept
as the murderous scene
unfolded, searing
my ears and eyes,
and decried that life
could never be
as before
until a plain bird
no larger than a leaf
alighted near
an open window,
sang a joyful song,
then flew.

Bob Goos — Maple Ridge, British Columbia, Canada
HOPE SHATTERS

sweating, scrabbling
hands torn and bleeding
digging, don't give up
somewhere a heart beats
a spirit lives
can't turn back
tear streaked
scrabbling in the rubble

and then
hope shatters with a crash
dust swirling
weight falling
life sucking
going down
death circling
no hope

but then a light appears
in the haze
from the cloud
a hand reaches
hold on!
      hold on!
            hold on!
a voice speaks
I reach and grasp
      strong hand
      drags me up

flesh suddenly touches
my other hand
another person
down there
reaching for the light
hold on!
      hold on!
            hold on!
hands grasp
and hold
coughing
gagging
we follow
the pinpoint of light
hand in hand
into light
      into life

I look around
      search the crowd
but none hold a flashlight
no familiar hand
to shake
two now live
because someone said
hold on
      in the darkness
hold on
      to each other
hold on
      back into the light

Kim Grove — Toronto, Ontario, Canada
STOP THE FREE FALL

On September 1 1, as television
etched into our memories
the image of two planes
knifing the trade towers
I found my thought go into free fall

The planes were missiles in the mind
Imploding ideas of hostility and hatred
I didn't even know for whom
The aggressive antagonism I felt
Was quickly heading me for
Ground zero

I had to stop the free fall
Ease up on the throttle of thought
Take control of my thinking
Use any energy to reclaim a sense of peace
Take my pulse off the panic button
Reflect on Life in its eternal nature
Take moments in the day
To find my equilibrium

And navigate my thoughts back to God.

Trish Shields — Courtenay, British Columbia, Canada
PIECES

he sits there   barely breathing
     a light dusting of ash sitting on
   his helmet   his face
partially covered by a mask
   his eyes glazed over from the
 work he has done   the work he
      still has waiting for him.

sirens echo off the shattered remains
    of the world trade center
and as the world holds its breath
     a small tear makes a path   down
        his grizzled chin
and onto hands that have touched
    cold brick   and   cold flesh.

   his shift is almost up   for today

but he knows   sleep is just something
  he used to do   as images of friends
   found in the rubble linger just
behind eyes that have seen too much
      on this eleventh day
        of September.

Sue Chenette — Toronto, Ontario, Canada
THAT EVENING

One bakes,
in her oven-warm kitchen
leans her weight
into the floury dough,
presses and turns it,
releases and folds,
shaping round loaves.

       sudden plane   flameslash blooming

One walks his dog,
follows around
their usual route,
then makes the loop again,
welcomes the jar of one heel
and then the other,
pacing over asphalt.

      from windows   plummet   they are holding hands

One irons,
soothing washday glide,
soft familiar hiss of steam.
She smooths a blouse,
a yellow tablecloth,
back and forth, back and forth,
regular as rocking.

     pluming   crumble   rubble   dust

Riva Dunaief — Boynton Beach, FL, USA
TERRORIST ATTACK

Winter is early this year.
    It must be winter.
The streets are full of snow,
    city snow, gray, lumpy
with trash disappearing under
    an avalanche of snow
falling from hot black clouds.
    The heat is freezong.
It must be freezong. People
    are congealed in gray ice,
crushed and broken under
    the Jihad glacier.

Viki Ackland — London, Ontario, Canada
YESTERDAY

I was alive
yesterday
full of hope
marveling at my
new job
great view
coffee steaming
at my desk,
surrounding by
decent strangers

my parents fretted
at my being
in New York
"muggers"
they whispered
I was not government
I have no power
I am one girl
like millions of
innocent

I lived my life
filled with hope
and compassion
I dreamt of a better world
I cried when I
watched atrocities
I mourned the children
I respected
my neighbor
I was not the devil

I was beginning
I was alive yesterday

Jeremiah Gilbert — Angelus Oaks, California, USA
BLACK BOX

The towers seem red from this altitude,
as if already ablaze by the fire of our landing.
How did we reach so high?
Did we not think of falling?
I will go before you, test the waters,
so that our descent will be smoother
than our rise from the ash to the realization
of our inevitable fall. But we will
be remembered, though returned to ash,
once they discover our black box.

John B. Lee – Brantford, Ontario, Canada
THE DAY THE PLANES FLEW IN

The day the planes
flew in
like fireballs
twin towers fell to dust
collapsing to a crush
of dream.
And people of an ancient ash
as primitive as chiseled stone
emerged in weirdly silent
gauzy groups ghosted by smudge
as widows in our midst
do sometimes dress themselves in grief.
And there upon that fatal island
all our loss
was gathered like a cindered cloth
that someone shook
to shroud the burning mountain
of our sorrow in.
The clarifying isinglass
of milky air
divides us as an
isotherm might spin its
unseen silk upon a loom of wind
and we are of a single weather
pole to pole.

In Washington
a tiny klatch of chambermaids
are gathered chatting in the street
outside a grand hotel
as empty as a hollowed gourd

and in that sweet-ache circle
the language breaks upon
the tongue
as seed-loving birds might crack
the shell of seeds
to make a fertile field
beneath a future flight

and what it means
is in the drift of breath
and blow of skirt
and what it means
is in the weep of weeds
when they are over-wet
and what it means
is in the way we hold the past
unfolding precious handkerchiefs
in which we keep
gold rings, dried flowers
a wisp of infant hair

grandfather's rusted gun.

John B. Lee — Brantford, Ontario, Canada
THE PHOTOGRAPH IS ACTUALLY THAT OF DAVID PEEL

'everything is everything'

Gravity is a predicament.
When we die standing
we fall.
The shock of it suddenly goes
deep in the earth
as moles seeking to solve
impossible tangles
of subterranean trees might also find
the difficulty in stone
the seep of soak
the slow collapse of sand
with the weight of someone walking
the smaller darkness.
And if by dogs
if by foxes
the star-nosed shrike of the soul
should go below farm-well fathoms
to push lost labyrinths
beyond a wet line
he'll flood himself floating
as it is with storm sewer and river swell.
And we find that home
is amazing peril...
the soap is waiting underfoot and foolish
the radio frays its chord
blue fire belches and blooms
the foxglove releases its garden digitalis
into the bitter tea of an aching heart
the apple pips break white
and thin the blood
we do the dead man's float
for hours
stumbled in the beautiful suburban pool
our blond hair floating a lightless halo
as we sink
reflected apples
with the weight of nothing
bob above us where the mind belongs.

Elizabeth St Jacques — Sault Ste. Marie, Ontario, Canada
SEPTEMBER DEATHS

september deaths
longing to hear
just one songbird

cries erupt around the world on this day when flowers fell
terror thickens with black smoke
dreams lay crushed beneath debris
oh light of love hold to your breast each flower
torn by evil hands

dark sun
i hold your hand
in thick black smoke

Ruth E. Walker — Whitby, Ontario, Canada
WEIGHT

Absence moves across the tongue
lamenting
a lack of words
inhaling the dust
the black of smoke
a downpour of papers, plastic, glass
flame
gingerly we tread
each step an agonized pressure
tender, so tender
lifting the shattered layers
shifting the ruin
longing for sound
seeking your scent
on pillows, jackets, bits of fabric
we carry your image
reaching back
tasting salt.

Richard M. Grove — Toronto, Ontario, Canada
Be Still

Be still and know that I am God*
Be still and know that God is Love
Be still and know that I am loved by Love
If all the world would only
be still
for but one minute
they would know
that they live move
and have their being
in divine Love.

Psalm 46:10

Chapter Three
Of Elegies And Aftermath

Patrick Lane — Saanichton, British Columbia, Canada
SMALL ELEGY FOR NEW YORK

A small bird sings in the apple tree today
where the fruit hangs heavy in the heat.
The harvest is still weeks away.
He sings to leaves to shelter him,
that there be flowers, nests, and seeds,
that the sky he knows will always be the sky.
In New York far away the great fires burn,
yet what birds sing will stay the night to come
a few more hours. In the garden I am bound
by what I say as you are bound.
I pray for what I know,
that birds must sing among bright leaves,
that apples ripen toward the fall,
that we must hold what we are born to hold,
and all our weariness today
is just a stay against the hours.

Prayer is bird song in the garden far away
from the play of shadows fire makes.
The silence of the dead is what we own.
It's why we sing. The sky is clear today.
Go on, I hear my father say, my mother too,
and though they rest in quiet graves
I hear them still. The sky is clear today.
The dead sing too in the wreckage and the fires.
We must listen to their song.
The burden is our lives.
We pray because we cannot turn away.

Katherine L. Gordon — Rockwood, Ontario, Canada
WANTING A WALL

Oh Jerusalem I envy you your wailing wall
Some public place anointed by the ages
where grief is vented, blessed
and taken up from the sufferer
into porous stone that holds
the tears of centuries
releasing slowly
tragedy transformed
to lessons in life.

There is no place to offer this hurt
to lay or leave it
no way to leaven wisdom from bitter bread,
passages into purgatory go unmarked.

Seen with reddened eyes
the colour of happiness past
the fog-bound future with its blackened edges
boundaries squared into small earth cell
inside a circle of failed promise.

William Gough — Toronto, Ontario, Canada
WTC AFTERMATH

Visceral ranting floods emotional valley
Asea in odious pools of septic rage
Permeating all mental meanderings
Diluting streams of innate innocence .

Turning skywards with ineffable yearning
Ascending the pinnacle of forgiveness
Evokes defiant flow of courageous tears
Cleansing solvent for ingrained animosity.

Salvatore Amico M. Buttaci — Lodi, New Jersey, USA
IN THE MADNESS OF A MORNING

I will remember you
for as long as I live
though your footsteps
are silent now

once I could know you
by the sound of your walking
I could expect soon
there would be laughter

who would've believed
our world would change
that in the madness of a morning
I would lose you

in the clearing of smoke
in the smoldering ashes
the small voice of hope
says only this: Life goes on

I will remember you
for as long as I live
though your photographs
are all I have

who would've thought
death could force itself
upon our joy
hush forever the kindest heart
the patter of footsteps
laughter loud as song
echo down the twists and turns
of my courage

I will never forget you
I will live on
though I walk alone
I will be strong

Jane Cassady — Syracuse, NY, USA

FOR NEW FRIENDS ALMOST LOST IN THE CONVERSA-TIONAL AFTERMATH

I can't tell the story
without mentioning
that you left so fast
you forgot
your endearing yellow sweater.

Our September is a countdown
from thunderclap to lightning,
and we may be too new

to withstand this magnification
of our darks and lights.

But I've learned since then
that what the desert's missing
is the pleasant smell of decay,
that the line is often blurred
between mandala
and ashtray, and I often make things worse
instead of better.

So I'm left alone with this
reproachful heap of yellow yarn.
I gather it up like lightning feathers,
hide it somewhere safe,
and pray for the return of
nihilism, innocent as dawn.

David E. Cowen — Houston, Texas, USA
MID MORNING COFFEE: ELEVEN DAYS AFTER

All is normal;
small clusters of conversation
cozy at half tables;
steam rising from white foam in brown cups;
half eaten scones forming layers of crumbs
on bent napkins.

Then there is a flash;
it bounces off every wall.

Dark eyes glance around
intersecting with others;
an unspoken fearful question exchanged.

A young girl with a pony tail, blushing,
puts a disposable camera back into a black bag
on the floor.

The vapors rise again
with nervous voices and muffled laughter;
nothing to worry about.

But we all know,
we are not the same.

We have been changed;
we have been changed.

Dave Waddell — Chesley, Ontario, Canada
SUN, BIRDS, SKY

The sun broke up and the sky became
quilted like cloth on a large frame,
quilted like maple wood in the tree;
Then the breeze arose
and the sky became so dark that I could see,
where the sky was least the birds swam;
Then the wind just stopped like an accident
and the sky rolled off like a sea.

Albert DeGenova — Oak Park, IL, USA
MOURNING

pole
like the lonely muffled tick

of a chrome Zippo lighter
open-close, click-click, click-click
uneasy fingers, hands in pockets
dark silhouette
on a lampless moonless half-mast corner
black hat pulled low
over black eyes that suffer
pride and power
those unrepentant prodigals.

click-ching
click-ching
or is it
silver chain against golden censer
incense burning before the requiem
click-ching
click-ching
the American flag
hangs its head
    the smoke
        the smoke.

Jeremiah Gilbert — Angelus Oaks, California, USA
AFTERTHOUGHTS

If I whisper, will you hear me?
A strand of breath about your cheek
As the words fall to oblivion.

If I shine, will you see me?
A glow about your fingertips
As my soul alights.

If I bleed, will you kiss me?
A scarlet smear across your lips
Tinting you with life.

If I lie, will you believe me?
Tell you there is meaning
As the world descends.

If I soar, will you catch me?
Glide upon my waxen wings
Till the feathers ignite.

If I cry, will you hold me?
The limitation of language reached
There is nothing left to say.

Cecilia G. Haupt — Altadena, California, USA
NO TWILIGHT HOURS

As the day catapults into night
there are no twilight hours
only bright sun into nocturnal black.
Mornings I touch cold crystals of dawn.
Open windows wide.
Fresh air blows through my house.
I smooth my barely ruffled bed.
I prepare my night fires;
Trim my lamps I no longer light.
The fractured minutes of my life
Fall into a clock-wise form.
Claustrophobic darkness. No transition
from shadowing sun to pale rising moon.
I stare at crackling stars
of a cold and lonesome night.

The beautiful mischief or our love
eclipsed by your death
has me calling you from room to room.
A photograph is not enough.

Ron Lamkin — Gaeta (LT), Italy
AMERICAN HEROES

Heroes on Flight 93
You knew that it was your time
No thought did you give to yourselves
For you knew your lives you must give

Three terrorists had control of the plane
Their intent was sinister
It was plain
Beasts were these three

Yet from the passengers rose
Men and women of courage and strength
Born and raised in these United States
Nourished by freedom and liberty

Like the minutemen of Concord fame
No hesitation did you make
No reward did you want
No remorse did you show

The faithful passengers rebelled
Defying Satan's plan
Giving the ultimate sacrifice
For a nation already in mourning

I salute each one of you
Who with daring and grace
Faced the sinister plot
And gave of yourselves

Let not your names be forgotten
Let the nation raise your battle flag
Let us meet your, our enemy
Let us vanquish what was begot.

Gabriel Rosenstock — Dublin, Ireland

MONSTROUS IN ISOLATION

There lies the daddy-long-legs
Dead on the windowsill
Two legs in the air stiff
On this September morning.
Magnified over and over again
They could be the Twin Towers.
Nostradamus did not speak of this death.
What is daddy-long-legs
In Latin, in French, in Arabic, in Hebrew, in ...
In Irish it is snáthaid an phúca,
The pooka's needle.
And what is a pooka if it exists at all?

A devil? A mischievous sprite? A dybbuk?
Something too old for this world, I suspect,
Something grown monstrous in utter isolation.

Todd Swift — Paris, France
AND THAT IT HAPPENED. HERE

In Memoriam: the victims of terror, September 11, 2001

And that it happened. Here.
And that it did, in September.
Here, it happened, and now.
And in this nation, that it was.

Land and air, it was, and many.
Dead it was and more than that.
How did it? - and many suffered.
None expected, though many did.

Never to not know it coming, but.
And that it came at once and often.
Across air - and right in the eye of all.
Many are dead, and then more dying.

Fall when it happened, and the falling.
Out of towers, out of doors, this year.
Darkness from fire, with fear so many.
O, that it was not-nothing - but was.

That it happened, and that some froze.
Were frozen at screen, phone, terminal.
The air froze and none flew or moved.
And that nothing could be other done.

That done, perishing, can never undo.
Terrible, done. And nothing instead.
On this land - now - the plenty, gone.
In our year, saw it - saw what can go.

More to come, not known, yes maybe.
And now the news - what now, tell me.
That it was here and there and people.
In places, like something else   or war.

And not saying or being able to send news.
All frozen, busy and much moving, ended.
That it did happen, in our year, in this nation.
That this did not ever unfold   we befriended.

Tall buildings, large planes, many structures.
Upended, closed, enshrouded   all billowing.
That it was not another thing   a flowering.
Instead of this intelligence, horror calculated.

At this time, no more to say, silence, for them.
Dead and triaged, in low streets, the separated.
Not to be divided, but to remain calm, he said.
Mayors and all grim stations praying for an end.

Mary Langer Thompson — Canoga Park, California, USA
THAT DARK DAY OF SEPTEMBER 11, 2001

We cruise out on the lake,
our slip partner absent,
set anchor in Papoose Bay.
My newspaper is in my lap and
the warm vinyl is comforting,
holding me up.

I stare at the water.
A lone duck swims across
a path of sunlight.
I remember light travels
slower in water
than in air.
Today seems like a good day
to slow down light,
maybe reach over the side
and grasp some.

J.Lindsay Kellock — Ottawa, Ontario, Canada
IN MEMORIAM

The image imprinted on my daughter's heart was a photo in Tuesday's newspaper of a man on fire, leaping from an office tower on fire.

The image that seized my heart, painted by my mind, was of six people, hands clasped, jumping from the office tower. I saw a young woman among them, a mane of taffy hair rising behind her, as they sank.

The sounds that tore at minds and hearts, through thousands of cell phones, echo and echo:

We've been hi-jacked, we're going to crash, it's too late, I love you, I love you so much.

Mom, something's happened, something hit the other building, oh no, Mom, I love you;

Still all right for now, we're going down the stairs ... it's more crowded now ... we can't get out, I can't get out.

All the cell phones ringing, heard and not heard, never forgotten. Daily lives torn up and away, bleeding, ripped, sheared into fragments, fused, shattered to thick, dark dust.

Charlotte Mair — British Columbia, Canada
CRY FOR THE WORLD

Cry for the refugees of Kosovo
For the children of India — shed a tear
Weep for the internment of the Japanese
For the hunger, the pestilence
The fear
and cruelties of humanity
towards humanity
Tear my heart out

The cleansing of the Jews
The hatred of a colour   the African
Irish folk who fathomed more than stormy seas
Tears flow freely for Poland's orphans
Flood victims of Chile, I weep 10,000 tears
Railroad tracks rusted in China's blood, sweat and tears
All these cruelties
Tear my heart out!

The lady of the night, caught in her unwanted vise
A lonely bag lady   pushing her basket of vacant dreams
While abused children cry out in vain
And I cry out in pain!

And I will never understand
So - called human beings of this earth
As I march to the beat of my own private heart
With each step of my life
Trying to change what I can
Still   I cry for the sake of my fellow man

Jeffrey Alfier — Tucson, AZ, USA
THE TEREBINTH

This gambling wilderness
where days become tangled
in a scion of stone
where new ravens whisper

polemics of fire
for an obdurate god
that dried the very wings
of these fallen sparrows.

We inherit shadows
as days become tangled
in the scion of stone.
That tree of Absalom.

Dina E. Cox — Unionville, Ontario, Canada

ONLY QUESTIONS

September 11, 2001
    you left us   alone

left us to ask our questions
of the wind, the answers
carried away   muffled
by still ballooning clouds
of dust, euphemism

for the unspeakable

flesh vaporized
in an instant of ineradicable images
of aeroplanes slicing
tall buildings as a knife

      might slice a throat
      or a birthday cake
      or water...

now part of clotted sweat falling
from the labouring foreheads
of emergency workers
attempting the impossible

dust   flesh   grit
thoughtlessly brushed from weary eyes
only to be breathed in - mark that!

inhaled in some sort
of cruel joke
those who search ingesting
the essence of what they search for...

> Does "e" still equal
> mass times velocity
> squared? Is the object
> of the search also the energy
> which spurs them on?

"no blood" the papers whisper
only concrete and steel
and this pervasive dust

can they feel our sadness
who are gone forever?

Richard M. Grove — Toronto, Ontario, Canada

THE NEXT TIME

The next time that you dress in the morning
and rub your tired face peering into the mirror
at the blur looking back at you,

The next time that you reach for your orange juice
and forget to kiss your kids
while you reach for your briefcase in numb banality,

The next time that you sneer with smug superiority
at a street person or judge with disdain by crossing the street
to save diverting your eyes in avoidance,

Remember the 11th of September 2001
and give pause to the equality of all mankind.
Drink in the precious aroma of now
by turning back to the moment
that you almost let slip away.
Be grateful that you are alive
that the entire world learned a lesson of brotherhood
unfortunately at the price of thousands.

Susan Ioannou — Toronto, Ontario, Canada
CROSSING

Now as you walk toward the falling light
leaving the path, for leaf dapple

nothing can turn your feet, nor stop
your soft dissolve into air

a shiver not quite caught in the eye
—yet there

as if in an atom's whirling spaces
is fullness beyond prayer

and aching after your absence
we touch you everywhere.

Maynard Luterman — Buffalo, New York, USA
IF THEY HAD KNOWN

if they had known
it was to be the last
day of their lives
would they have watched
the sun stretch
and rise from its sleep
would the clouds
have been sails
launched across a
matisse sky
would they have
heard the wind
strum the trees
or the birds singing
arias by bach
and mozart
would goodbye have been
a loving
tearful hug
and a kiss from god
and how many
would have said
i am sorry

in the ruins
i watched the ghosts
dance upon my dreams
as ton upon ton of rubble
was heaped on the fabric
of their lives
i could hear their surprise
and taste their tears
their innocence and
all of ours
stained red
i watched them
march to where their
hearts broke
questions asked that
had been forgotten
we saw ourselves
in their suffering
and knelt and said
thank you
as we learned that
in holding
you are held
and in loving
you are loved

as for vengeance

it is not wine
it will grow
bitter with time

Kathleen Kemp Haynes — Dorchester, Ontario, Canada
UNTITLED

Mass Murder
body parts,
how vulnerable.
how violated these members
of the dead.
a watch on an arm,
last inspected
to time a meeting
or a coffee break.
how can we ever
put sanity back
into a world so
wrong-side-out?
when will the birds
that fly appointed routes
again retain confidence
of safe arrival?
the whole world
looks on at this site
of carnage and fear
and can't stop seeing.
when will reason
and peaceful life
ever return?
when the captains and the kings
depart, who will look after
the children?

Penn Kemp — Toronto, Ontario, Canada
ALTAR EGO

Something has happened to
the I on this passage. I is
no longer a point of view,
stuck to this emotion or that,
the site of accumulated
experience. I has shed
the necessity of self defense.
I is a floating centre of perception.

I has widened to include
you and you and you be-
cause no barrier intrudes
between us.

I has become compound,
many-faceted. Complexity
leaps to a larger simpler
system. I is surprised
the words continue even
here. I is resting in
a continuum Am.

The diphthong of pain
Aeiii ground down
to seed syllable AUM.

Have you noticed that if you stay
with an image long enough
the fear you felt dissolves
into a live love you can embrace?

Joan McGuire — Orangeville, Ontario, Canada

SEPTEMBER 11, 2001

What was is gone,
flame blasts crashing
over a gasping world,
screaming rubble and tears.

Some cling to fading hopes,
some plan angry retribution
against an amorphous foe,
some call out to their god.

Others, in stunned disbelief,
watch, wordless, as horror
silences the voice,
stills the poet's pen.

Achingly beautiful, this sunshot
morning. Monarch butterflies
flitter among asters. Fleeting,
a hummingbird hovers,

and is gone. Wild geese
sound haunting cries
as they head south
over America's sorrow.

Lee Schwartz — New York, NY, USA
WIRELESS

"I love you,"
"Get me out of here!"
"I'm making my way down,"
"What's happening I can't see?"
Last recorded syllables
of loved ones about to die.
Some knew these were
their final words on earth.
Some hoped to see family
soon on the ground.
Messages from the 84th floor,
Hymns from the 110th floor,
pleas from the 79th floor,
vowels of love and thank you,
breath of bittersweet memory,
music of life carried through
digital air bounced off antennas.
Racing to reach a beloved soul
and seal their final thoughts before
they were no longer of this earth
but joined to the digital air and magnetic
fields of magic amulets.

P.K. Page — Victoria, British Columbia, Canada
FORGIVE US

Forgive us, who have not
been whole or rich as fruit;
who, through the eye's lock, enter
a point beyond the centre
to find our balance shot;

who have, if we confessed,
observed, but never guessed
what lies behind the fact:
the quiet, incipient act
that alters all the rest.

Those of us who took
the style to be the book,
the incident as all
and unequivocal,
must take another look.

Our blueprint was at fault.
The edifice we built
disintegrates and falls;
haunting its ruined halls
the spectre of our guilt.

That kindergarten ghost
is suddenly our host
and, once we're wined and dined,
wants to be paid in kind
and fast becomes our guest.

Chapter Four
Weeds Of War
Blossoms Of Brotherhood

Joan Latchford — Toronto, Ontario, Canada
FRONTAL ATTACK

I will be the first to welcome you
to the neighbourhood,
bring a pizza on moving day
for a covenant of salt.

I will be the first to speak
in the elevator,
draw others to admiration
of your son's beauty.

And if, oh my enemy
my love is misplaced,
perhaps you will suffer
a moment of regret –

as you seal the envelope.

Dave Waddell — Chesley, Ontario, Canada
COINS

I come in the lane and I go out again;
I pass you on the road and you pass me on the road;
I eat in the restaurant and you eat from a lunch bag in your car;
I go to work and I build furniture and you go to work and you build snow
blowers;
I go to my home and you go to your home;
I read the news and you read the sports section;
I go to bed at night and get up in the morning my way and you go to bed and
get up in the

morning your way;
How can we be alike for we are different;
How can we be different because we are alike;
I look in the mirror and I see myself;
You look in the mirror and you see yourself.

I.B.Iskov — Thornhill, Ontario, Canada
PEACE

United
And happy
As like two elephants
With a lineage
Of jaffa
Of emeralds
Of rose petals
In a population of kodak guns

Arms join with other
Arms create the gesture
Warm branching
The first
Tree

Numbers erased by the light
Of the universe
Courses
Into the Dominion
Flag by flag
Made from trees
And ivory.
Cities share metallic lessons
Large spaces without gravity
Keep quiet blind complicity
Without attitude or prejudice

The free grain
Multiplies at will
The children of the meadow
Fill the world with numbers
On wings of stone
Soar over the seasons
And race with the tide
Arm in arm

The roots of all things
And their universe
Will be firmly transplanted in neon
In gestures
In joys
In peace

Stephen Humphrey — Toronto, Ontario, Canada
SPECIAL FORCES FOR THE RECONSTRUCTION

The new special forces come
    not with guns
but construction equipment
    armies descend on the villages
with public works contracts
      while jets overfly
     littering seeds on the ground
      meanwhile prisoners
are led into the desert
    to be shown
the birthplace of the Devil
       and God
to meet the holy spirit
    in a helix of sand

This method of warfare proves strategically sound
    for the population
      always surrender.

Bernice Lever — Bowen Island, British Columbia, Canada
SWORDS ARC NO RAINBOWS

Warships improve no sunsets
Smart missiles give no milk white
Nerve gas paints no blossoms yellow
Bombs grow no living green
Explosions share no sky blue
Rockets create no twilight purple
Bullets donate no blood red
Tanks pulp no juice orange
Terrorists smile no lips pink

Free will to choose:
grey ash, death's black charcoal
or God's pure gold of love.

Bernice Lever — Bowen Island, British Columbia, Canada
OLDIES

Have You Ever
Have you ever thought
that the blind
have no colour prejudices
and the deaf care
not for speeches, etc.,

but even lacking our five
over-rated senses,

people have the choice
to hate   or
to love?

Bernice Lever — Bowen Island, British Columbia, Canada
PRAYER

I don't want to live everyday
as the last day,
grasping and clasping
at disintegrating care
    like a fish leaping
    from an oil slick
    into our polluted air.

Grant me the wisdom
to live each day
as the first day,
    shy in its newness
    strong in its promise.

Charlotte Mair — British Columbia, Canada
QUICKENING

There's definitely something to the word fear

"We have nothing to fear but fear itself",
was the famous "FDR" line
and I love it!

Without fear, there is no room for courage
and without courage a human lacks strength
I don't want the comfortable way,
the sure way, the main stream forever
Sometimes we've got to trod down unversed paths;
Tarry on the back roads

With new found wisdom
I'll scale mountains and remove all doubt
as to what this life holds
I'll play the ball where it lands
Sink my self into matters of awakenings,
a quickening   yes, a quickening

Sharon Singer — Toronto, Ontario, Canada
PEACE

I ask how many
I ask how many among us
I ask how many among us have come to peace

Peace
we long for it, kill for it
peace in the world
peace in our hearts and souls
peace in our daily lives
in our families
peace at work

But peace
isn't a tangible
doesn't come in brown paper wrappings
like a gift
can't be bought or sold
or manifested with only a prayer
can't be bartered or put on deposit for dividends
can't be legislated
can't be won with shotgun threats
bruised black eyes, screams, nagging or murder.

We struggle
with inner battles
war against ourselves
fight in waking and
dream life
with enemies – bosses, spouses, soldiers, monsters –
all of whom are aspects
of ourselves

Accept the crippled self
love the foibles, faults and failures
embrace the ugliness, the shame
and love without reserve, unconditionally
more than your mother ever loved you

The road to peace is through
transformation
transillumination
transfiguration

For when we become translucid beings
who transfuse peace into the world like life's blood
then the universe will sing in harmony –
each with a different song
in a different key, on a different scale
but ah,
the music we will make

Frances Ward — Hamilton, Ontario, Canada
THEY SHOOT   THEY SCORE

they shoot   they score
we
watch   the replay
watch   the replay
watch   the replay

replay

learn about   the players
tour   the training camps
see   the fans cheering
meet   the head coach
wait for   the puck
to drop
on another   damn period
                  of overtime

Lorraine Geiger —
THE DAY AFTER

Abdul is a timid child.
He trembles in dark rooms,
in moving elevators,
and near television images.

Abdul is a grieving child.
He mourns the loss of his best friend's father.
feels his sorrow, his agony,
along with his own.

Abdul is a prayerful child.
He prays to God
to protect his family, his friend's family, and
America, his homeland.

Abdul is a fearful child.
He fears the stares of strangers,
the coldness of neighbors,
and the explosive graffiti
on his father's house.

Veronica Golos — New York, NY, USA
CANDLES BENEATH THE SAND

In the light of this dawn
Our hands are not enough.
We need the wide gesture of longing,
The ancient pose - of supplication.

Walk the sunrise, and remember.
Perhaps it will not happen tomorrow.
So, in your own mind, hold it;
Like a breath before you dive.

Trees fail, they've done all they can.
The years too, flicker, turn red, and fall.
How much weeping does the Willow do
Before it turns to something else?

The sea bell rocks and tolls
of landlocked sorrow
The world turns white; white and gray
Like ash, like foam, like bright glaring day.

The whales of living, sound, go down;
But they go down to joy - while we,
With our unbound feet, and feeling hands,
Suppose our joy; defy our grief.

Watch the candle's glow beneath the sand
Hear the wild keening of the leaves;
Do not let go this lovely earth
So worn with love   so passionate with us.

Karin de Weille — Yonkers, NY, USA
THE ASTONISHING TREE

No environment is too barren or too hostile–
hills, beaches, even roads.
The seed will hibernate beneath the surface for years–
as long as it takes–before it strikes out.
Germination, triggered by the first drop
of a human foot, and maturation into the full-grown invisible tree
is instant, as is the harvest which lies scattered about.
The split-apart fruit reveals no seed.
Here you have the most remarkable feature
of this fast-spreading tree and the secret
of its evolutionary success–its mechanism
of reproduction: it shoots its seed
into the hearts of men, who then disseminate it with
wonderful efficiency.

Joan McGuire — Orangeville, Ontario, Canada
THE TERRORIST

In the name of his god he is driven,
with a passionate conviction of right,
death the insignificant price
of his greater cause.

Smashed in a fury of religious fervour
the twin towers to mammon collapsed
into fiery rubble and screaming dust.

Through homes and shops
again and again
the scene replays,
searing minds,
blasting complacency,

and we who were sleeping
suddenly awake. What seemed
far away
is right here, and the unknown
foe, our greatest danger
and fear, may be the terrorist
we each harbor
within.

Susan Whelehan — Toronto, Ontario, Canada
SEPTEMBER'S LULLABY

When both my boys were babies I would go
Into their rooms at night. I could not sleep.
I'd walk amidst the sun and moon and stars.
I'd listen for their breath and feel sweet warmth
Upon my cheek. I'd brush loose baby curls
Across a forehead smooth and lotion- soft.
I'd watch their bellies rise and fall with life,
Then tuck the hand- made quilt in one more time
And know that they were safe and all was well.

As they grew up I learned to sleep at night.
They'd brush their teeth and snuggle as we read.
After the "Just one more?" we'd say our prayers.
They'd thank God for their cousins, Dr. Seuss,
The big, fat pigs at Riverdale Farm.
I'd kiss them both goodnight and that was that.
The world of dreams was ours to live within.

Now in the wake of jet-fuelled suicides,
Of terrorism waking in our land,
We brush and snuggle, pray and kiss and then
I cannot sleep. I go back to their rooms.
I walk amidst the posters of their teams,
Step over sweat pants, dirty socks, a ball.
I listen for their breath and feel sweet warmth
Upon my cheek. I touch the pizza sauce
his washcloth missed, and think, not long ago,
before it all, that would have upset me.
I shake my head and breathe in long and deep.
I breathe out prayers for courage, peace and sleep.

Magdolna Boda — Szeged, Hungary
GLADIATORS

The play is the same
And the spectators have not changed
Neither their hard features became older
Their eyes are sharp,
While spotlight is dazzling them.
Religions, huge monies
Their blood is up
And the gladiators,
Aeroplanes and towers
Wars, crusades and death and death
The mankind drops off like flies
Arena is here, arena is there
New York, Ethiopia, Bosnia
Each day the world is less and less
Diseases, hunger and aids
This other death is slow, slower
while the spectators are the same.

Richard M. Grove – Toronto, Ontario, Canada
BEYOND THE TERROR OF 9/11

As time goes on,
Remembr the terror,
but only in the vaguest way.
Remember the panic,
as only the short stop,
along your spiritual journey.
Remember the stark images,
only in the dimmest light,
as a reminder,
of how far we have come,
in the united brotherhood,
of forgiveness.
Remember the feelings
of heart break,
but let them fade,
from devastation to hope,
from fear to trust.
See beyond the anger of 9/11,
to mankind's redemption.
We will learn,
from this experience,
we will be lifted,
to resurrection,
through our dedication,
to love that will take us,
to forgiveness.

Soar above the Terror
on wings of forgiveness.

Kay Barone — Natick, Massachusetts, USA
OUR WORLD

"Mine," said the toddler, snatching the toy.
"Mine," said the king, counting the gold.
"Mine," said the explorer, finding new land.
"Mine," said the settler, brandishing a gun.
"Mine," said the home owner, fencing a yard.
"Mine," said the ruler, controlling the bomb.
"Gone," sighed the angel, flying over the void.

Penny L. Ferguson — Truro, Nova Scotia, Canada
WE WILL NEED THE WRITERS

The media says we will need the writers
to help us make sense of this.

I have had no desire
to give utterance
to this unspeakable horror...

But because we are called upon,
I jot down ideas–
reaching out to touch loved ones
for the final time;
the buildings melting like
cotton candy under a diabetic's tongue;
the arrogance to think
it couldn't happen here;
fighting a war with shadows;
the search for survivors/bodies
like searching for a ncedle
on a mountainside;
an impotent world wanting to help;
discussions leading my teenaged son
from wanting to kill them all
to forgiveness with rational justice;
my words to him if war comes,
as Christians, we will do
what we have always done:
be the best people we can
in whatever circumstances
we are given.
I turn these, and many more, ideas
over and over in my mind
like a child with a puzzle box.
I look for a way to comprehend
the incomprehensible,
for words to put on paper,
but nothing comes.

I wonder if my failure is denial
but I know this is not true.
I have viewed all of the footage,
taken part in all the discussions.

Then I realize it is my faith
that is my peace and salvation
from this aberration also—
the peace of knowing
however and whenever
I depart this planet
to be absent from the body
is to be present with the Lord.

Charlotte Mair — British Columbia, Canada
W—A—R

You make it easy
to leave this world
with your sardonicism

Spell it out
W—A—R
it reeks of melancholy
lacked faith
iron lunged
metal fatigued body snatchers
ancient black veils   stealing the new day dawn

War   gnashing, crashing machines

to scrape the innocent   grind and pupate minds
War and war again
will it end and who is the victor
when all is said and done
all losing
War

Robert Priest — Toronto, Ontario, Canada
TARGET PRACTICE

(the bull's eye)

the bull's eye is the scapegoat
minus its face
stripped of its uniform and nationality
no religion or name
it is the narrow telescopic end
of the mirror
an accidental twin you can't help
killing again and again,
immortal, eternal there in its circles

the bull's eye is the angel
you go hunting for
when winter comes yet again
it is a flock of fathers
finally made small
a round outlaw in hiding
zeroed in on
and paralyzed

it is the last civilian
the last tower
the last great symbol

the bull's eye
is your anger compressed
made efficient and holy
ringed by a dozen haloes
it is the bright erupting dot
of a hatred
that practice only makes
more perfect

Linda M. Stitt — Toronto, Ontario, Canada
DIVINE ORDER

For the sorrow of the world,
we must learn boundless compassion.
It can no longer be reserved
for blood or tribe or nation.

The grief that circles the globe
reminds us
we are one family.
Each starving child
is our child.

There is no Them,
there is only Us,
united in suffering,
evolving into awareness.

And if great horror does not teach us,
greater horror will anoint us
with realization

Jessica Arluck — New York, USA.
MIDTOWN SIRENS

I now pray for the sweet melody of loud sirens

the ambulance is my hope
the beautiful, proud noise
a possibility of survival
of a rescued father
a saved wife
a recovering hero

Tuesday, Wednesday, and Thursday
a chorus of sirens sang strong throughout the day
but Friday came with mostly silence
gloriously interrupted by hope a few times

the weekend came and went without sirens
I never knew the sound of war
could appear to be so dreadfully peaceful

Joshua Willough — Eden Mills, Ontario, Canada
PERILS AND DANGERS OF THE NIGHT

Orange bloom–
black over America:
New York is burning!

Dark strangers in the yard–
my window's cracked,
your door is jammed.

Black Jack's found out
where we live–
where the children go to school.

He occupies the captain's seat
of the ship that brings you home.

He walks down Wyndham Street–
maybe with a brown bag
under his arm–
umbrella raised.

He sees you waiting for the train–
he spits in your chicken soup.

His twisted blade whet
by your imagination–

mission accomplished–
he retreats
to Ali Baba's tent.

Carla Theodore — Woodville, Virginia, USA
THE HIGHJACKERS

Apparently you were not stupid,
    not desperate, ignorant or poor.
    I'm not even sure you believed
    God wanted you to get to heaven
    that way

    The part I just don't understand
    is that you lived among us for years
    and our American magic
    failed to penetrate
    the armor of your conditioning

    In the glow of friendship
    and approval
    I've seen hate sweeten
    and melt like wax
    of the honey bee.

    I've seen stiff and proper immigrants
    become artists in the subversive air
    of our anarchy.
    What made you so impervious?

    I think you must have been robots.
    For robots don't care if they live or die
    and they can be programmed
    to kill.

    Maybe you saw the passengers eyes
    riveted upon you,
    but since you had no hearts
    you were undeterred
    even by the widened eyes of a child.

    I want to think you were robots
    for how can we accept
        that you belonged to us
        – the family of man?

Ruth E. Walker — Whitby, Ontario, Canada
NATURAL DISASTER

You fear the catastrophe
heaving tectonic plates, raging
winds, thundering rains
rising oceans
shifts in polarity
asteroids falling, aliens
invading, the sun exploding
      the universe
      imploding
      the absence of God:
But it is the hand at the stick
eyes on a distant horizon
that brings it all home.

Caroline H. Davidson — Pickering, Ontario Canada
SIMPLE THINGS

I am washing the dishes
listening to the news
kitchen TV shows flames
smoke, haggard firemen
with blackened faces

my hand moves the sponge
over the white plate
follows the curved pattern
pushes the soap bubbles
over the smooth centre

too hard to imagine
the noise of sirens
crashing bricks and steel
screaming men and women
running toward the camera

soap bubbles smooth a cup
my hand pushes the sponge
around the inside cleaning
coffee and cream smudges
watching a fireman's dirty face

James Deahl — Hamilton, Ontario, Canada
WRITTEN IN TIME OF WAR

Grapevines rattle their leaves at my window
    with the sound of autumn.
The DOFASCO works casts blue shadows
    into a bluer harbour.
Sumacs speak outside the rolling mill
    of the coming frost.

In other cities, far, far away,
    people are torn apart.
Death emerges from skies blackened
    by the screams of jet engines.
Later, a cool dawn emerges
    from mountain passes.

October is a thousand scarves
    tattered by long winds.

Chris Buczkowski — Lockport, NY, USA
BETWEEN SEVENTY SEVEN AND FIVE

An executive.
New job, new city.
His family had moved to the east coast,
they wouldn't be apart.
Somehow in moving they had forgotten the dog
so he went.
Purchased the ticket,
boarded the plane.
Traveling with the best intentions.
Retrieving his best friend,
a Yellow Lab.
As his plane flew into the pentagon.

Katerina Fretwell — Parry Sound, Ontario, Canada
THE HUMBLING

That mushroom cloud
bloomed in Manhattan
streets too silent
save footsteps
all running for life

Life means nothing
human firebombs
turning America
against Americans

Americans forced
kamikaze
imploding world trade
and military supremacy

Supremely, Anise
Graves funereal
"America The Beautiful"
voiced all the violence
mourned every victim

Victim of false pride
Manhattan my
birthplace but Graves
"America" humble
has room for me

"Me" swept aside while
heroes around & against
the clock – mucked
the mushroom mountain
seeking the living

Living under the cloud
zero ground
safety's illusion
blown apart   too hard to
live with that

Wendy Webb — Norfolk, UK
MASADA SHALL NOT FALL AGAIN

Yesterday, a Kamikaze was a 'hero',
a cause to die for,
a war to end all wars.
Trading his life for heaven on earth,
a martyr hanging medals from his soul.

Today, a War Veteran paused,
a minute's silence for the dead,
as mobile phones screamed last goodbyes,
white hankies pleaded truce,
and dawn on the Big Apple smoked like Dante's Inferno.

Tomorrow, world leaders wait on the President,
Air Control suspended from busyness.
The silence of World Trade
as New York bleeds a fortress in the sky.
Earth breathes a new Masada - and sanity asks, Why?

*Previously published in "Nursing Creature of the Deep" Wendy Webb (UK),
poetry collection, October 2001.*

Wendy Webb — Norfolk, UK
HAIKU

Mushroom planes revenge,
Choking despair, courage, trade.
West, insane, meets East.

Michele M. Gallagher — San Antonio, TX, USA
WE ARE ALL ON TRIAL

Yes   jurisdiction surrounds us.
Collective souls being sworn in.
Substantial evidence piles the desk.
Venerated judge contemplating our fate.

Revenge, the highly publicized goal.
Leader driving hard to strike back.
Wrath overpowers common logic.
Highest priority now, is hate.

Yet this land is loved by many.
Who've labored in great pains.
Red wine, green cash, gold dancing.
Ordinary smiles now turning to rain.

How is it this shocks our spirits?
Years of arrogance have finally collapsed.
I support the Intellectual solution:
Understanding what caused these effects.

Because there is no need for more bleeding.
Babies dead. Men & Mothers share grief.
Counter-attacks, slaughter NOT the answer.
Security will flow when the judge rules in peace.

All of us are on trial this morning & night.
Every person, everywhere, in some form.
Together, we decide what will happen.
How and when this world of ours will change.

Of course, we can again choose destruction.
But what will this, our children, teach?
Instead open minds   diversity is wise.
Develop as better humans   being.

Yes, awaiting verdict, we can aid success.
Hands & mouths of compassion. 1000 smiles blessed.
Dialogue to occur, exclusively from this point.
Humanity will grow. But first we plant the seeds.

The alternative is death. Life covered in darkness.
Jurisdiction surrounds us, as a group.
What do you wish for tomorrow?

DO NOT WEEP

When I go do not weep
Look at the beauty of trees
And listen to a bird's song
For my spirit is never gone
Happy memories always keep